W9-BST-838

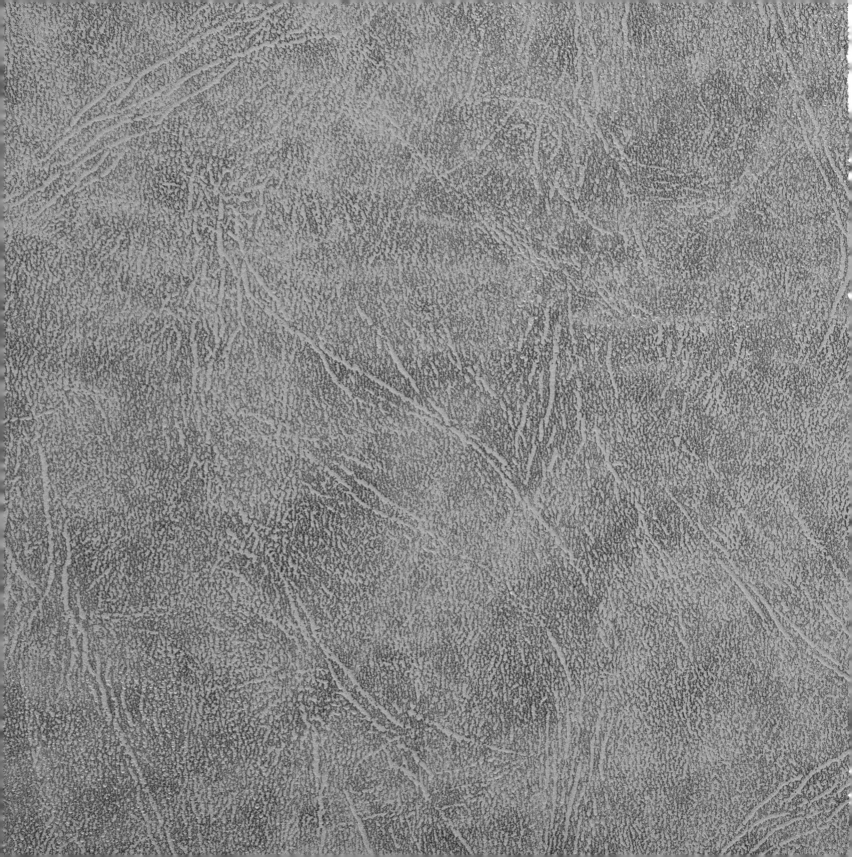

# I Am Africa

Carl R. Sams II & Jean Stoick

# Acknowledgements

We would like to thank our loyal staff: Karen McDiarmid, Becky Ferguson, Bruce Montagne,
and Sandy Higgins for their contributions in the creation of this book.
Thanks to Laura Sams, Rob Sams, Jennifer Cowen, Rachel Ferguson, Lauren Ferguson,
Bridget Llewellyn, Hugh McDiarmid and Erick Whitford for their contributions.
Thanks to Phyllis Brantingham and the students of Spring Mills Elementary School for their ideas.
Thanks to Doug Peterson for the cover design.
Thanks to Greg Dunn for his artistic contribution.
Thanks to Lou & Donna Waldock for introducing us to Africa.

Copyright ©2014 Carl R. Sams II & Jean Stoick — All Rights Reserved.

No part of this book may be reproduced in any manner without the authors' expressed
written consent, except in the case of brief excerpts in critical reviews and articles.
Inquiries about this book should be addressed to:

Publisher

**Carl R. Sams II Photography, Inc.**

361 Whispering Pines

Milford, MI 48380

800/552-1867   248/685-2422   Fax 248/685-1643

www.strangerinthewoods.com    www.carlsams.com

Karen McDiarmid — Art Director

Sams, Carl R.
I Am Africa
by Carl R. Sams II & Jean Stoick, Milford, MI
Carl R. Sams II Photography, Inc. © 2014

Printed and bound February 2014 — #200429
Friesens of Altona, Manitoba, Canada

ISBN  978-0-9827625-6-1

Animals; Mammals; Birds; Africa
Library of Congress Control Number:  2014931139

10 9  8 7 6 5 4 3 2 1

Summary: Children of all ages will enjoy exploring this rich
tapestry of ecosystems, teeming with wildlife, as they discover
who should claim the title, "I Am Africa".

Dedicated to those who
protect wild places
and care for
wild things.

I am Africa.

I am the grass
growing tall in the savanna.
I hide the cheetah as she hunts prey
to feed her cubs.

I am the grass.
I hide the weak and vulnerable.
I provide for the hungry herds
migrating across the plains of Africa.

The birds of Africa
echo all the colors of
the rainbow.

We scatter
the seeds
throughout the savanna.

We are
"Insect Control Extraordinaire,"
a *most* necessary job!

We are Africa!

We are best buddies.

We climb trees
and play games of
"catch-me-if-you-can."

Are we Africa?

We are large and
our strength is in our numbers.
We are the elephant family . . .
we are Africa!

I am strong like a steamroller.
With my thick hide and pointy horn,
nobody challenges me.

I am the rhino.

I am Africa!

I am the starling. I am Africa!
I keep this rhino bug-free.

I appreciate the
crunchy insect treats
and the ride.
He's my traveling smörgåsbord.

Hey there warthog!
Do you need a
tick-check too?
You're next!

I am the termite hill
found throughout
all of Africa.

My shape can be elaborate
or simply . . .
a mound.

When the termites vacate,
I am a home for the
dwarf mongoose and
other small creatures.

I am the termite mound.
I offer a vantage point for
the predator . . .

. . . and for the
watchful prey.

I am Africa.

I am the lioness.

I hunt for the pride.
I had a most successful hunt at dawn.

But shhhh!
Don't tell the wildebeest.

I like to intimidate
and make them run!

I am Africa!

We are the curious giraffes.
　　With our long legs and towering necks,
　we watch over all things.

We oversee the
battling impalas and
observe the tiny dik-diks
weaving through
the grass.

We are Africa.

Who is Africa?
I don't know . . . but look,
here's a toy!

I saw it first!

No, no, no.
Mama said we have to share!

Many say we are the most dangerous
animal in Africa.

We are the hippos.

Our days are spent
submerged in water
to protect our hides from
the blistering sun.

We may look big and clumsy,
        but don't mess with us!
Our jaws are enormous and we *will* charge.
                    We are Africa!

Although I am a kingfisher,
I don't catch fish.
I prefer bugs.

We are the clever bee-eaters.
We capture stinging insects,
often in mid-flight.

We are Africa.

I am dust.
I cover the coats and hides of the animals.
Biting insects find me
most distasteful!

We are the zebra.
Our family travels in large herds.
Our many eyes watch for predators.

We are Africa.

Zebra foals
have brown stripes.

I want to keep
*my* brown stripes forever!

Dust and dirt!
Dust and dirt!
I *love* dust and dirt!

Splash and squirt! Splash and squirt!
Water is for splashing and squirting.

I *love* water!

Can we be Africa?

I am water, essential for all living things.

I am water that makes the rivers flow.

I create the deep swamps
and mud . . . glorious mud!

I am Africa.

I am mud!
I'm not made just for wallowing.
I keep insects from biting.

I am cooling
and soothing.
And I do wonders
for this fellow's
complexion.

I am the thick underbrush.

As the sun heats the day, mother leopard
and her cub seek my shade . . .
to rest and to sleep.

I grow green foliage
for the hungry gazelle
and other grazers.

I am Africa.

I am the crowned crane,
the crowned royalty of Africa.
Isn't it obvious?

My beauty and grace is pure
poetry in motion.

I am Africa!

I am the lion.
There is a reason
I am called the "King."

I am Africa . . .
and I look the part!

ROAR-RRR!

Wait!
WAIT!
WAIT!

Africa is
in *all* of you!

Everybody step back!
Pick a tick out of your fur
and be happy!

Together,
we are *all* a part of the bigger picture.

We *all* march to the beat
of the same drum.

Together, we are Africa!

Wildebeest

Leopard

Hippopotamus

Cheetah

Cape Buffalo

Warthog

Glossy Starling

Impala

Dik-Dik

Zebra

Giraffe

Lilac-breasted Roller

African Elephant

Bee-eater

Grey-headed Kingfisher

White Rhinoceros

Oryx

Female Lion

Male Lion

Crowned Crane

Hartebeest

Red-billed Oxpecker

Baboon